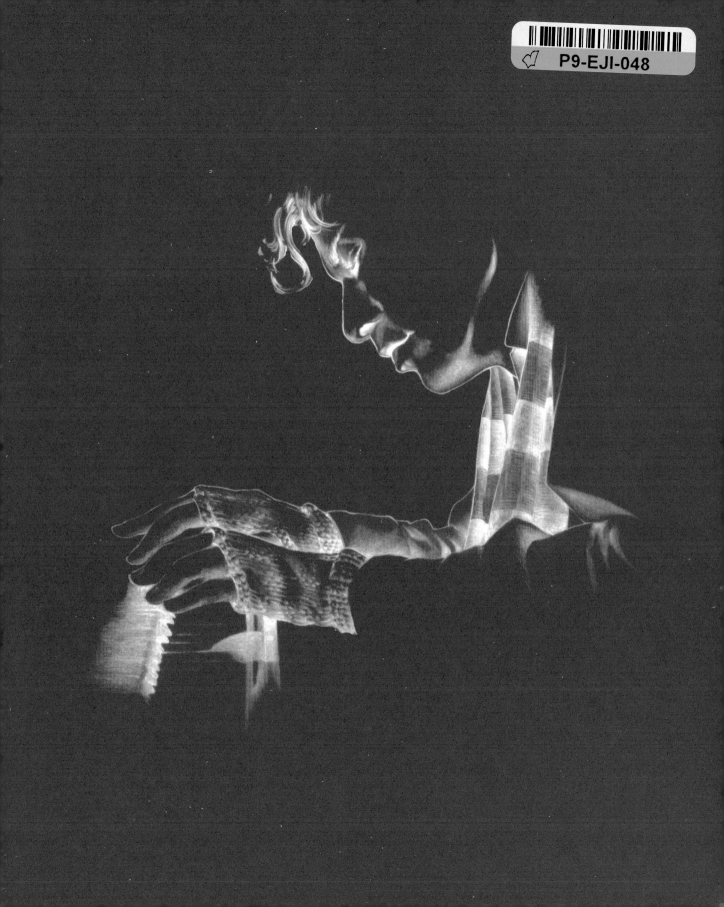

Struggling
for Perfection

The Story of Glenn Gould

Stories of Canada

Struggling for Perfection

The Story of Glenn Gould

Vladimir Konieczny

Illustrations by Chrissie Wysotski

series editor Allister Thompson

Napoleon Publishing

Napoleon Publishing
Toronto Ontario Canada
www.napoleonpublishing.com

Napoleon Publishing acknowledges
the support of the Canada Council for the Arts
for our publishing program.
Napoleon Publishing also acknowledges the support of
the Government of Ontario through the
Ontario Media Development Corporation's Ontario Book Initiative.

Le Conseil des Arts
du Canada
depuis 1957

The Canada Council
for the Arts
since 1957

Printed in Canada

National Library of Canada Cataloguing in Publication

Konieczny, Vladimir, 1946-
Struggling for perfection : the story of Glenn Gould / Vladimir Konieczny.

ISBN 0-929141-13-X

1. Gould, Glenn, 1932-1982--Juvenile literature. 2. Pianists--Canada--Biography--Juvenile
literature. I. Title.

ML3930.G696K82 2003   j786.2'092
         C2003-902841-0

A Musical Odyssey

The time capsules in Voyagers I and II include several sounds from Earth, including a declaration from then President Jimmy Carter and a series of greetings in various languages: the first in Sumerian, Earth's oldest known language, the last in English. There are also sounds of Earth: whales breathing, volcanoes rumbling, barking dogs, whistling trains, people laughing. As well, there is music from around the world, including Pygmy women from Zaire singing, a song by Louis Armstrong, a Japanese flute, an aria from a Mozart opera, and a wedding song sung by women from Peru.

Billions of kilometres from Earth, two spacecraft sail silently through inky space. Launched in 1977, Voyager I and Voyager II had passed the farthest known planet in our solar system by 1990. Inside each ship is a time capsule. Among the many messages to unknown civilizations, there is a recording of J. S. Bach's Prelude and Fugue in C Major from Book One of *The Well-Tempered Clavier*. The pianist is Glenn Gould.

If there are other intelligent beings in the universe, and they find our space ships, they will hear glorious music written by one of Earth's great geniuses and played by another. They may wonder about the musician who made the recording. What was he like? What did he do? What did he think about?

Many people have asked these same questions about Glenn Gould ever since he captured the world's attention. A thin, handsome man with pale brown hair, he fascinated people from the beginning of his career until his death in 1982, and still his legend grows.

A special human being, Glenn Gould was a gentle rebel who struggled for perfection in everything he did. He shared his music and his ideas about music with the world. He changed the way many people think about music.

You Who Are About to Leave

In the same year, 1964, the University of Toronto conferred an honorary Doctor of Laws degree on Glenn. Although he had never attended university, Glenn had by this time earned the respect of audiences and musicians around the world.

In 1964, Glenn spoke to the graduating students of the Royal Conservatory of Music in Toronto. He knew the place well, having studied there himself not so many years earlier when it was called the Toronto Conservatory of Music. The students listened quietly to his every word. Many were in awe of this famous young genius and probably hoped to be as successful someday.

On that day, Glenn spoke passionately about music. He stressed the importance of the imagination and encouraged his audience to recognize that the imagination is the place where all creative ideas are born.

Early in the speech, however, he said that if he could tell the room full of hopeful young musicians any one thing, it would be that they should not live too much by the advice of others. In other words, they should think for themselves.

From the time he was a little boy until his death, Glenn thought for himself. Sometimes he annoyed people with his ideas; other times he made them laugh, but more often than not he made people think. He was different. He knew he was, and everyone else knew it, too. Some people thought he was strange, but they simply didn't understand him. He lived a most unusual life on his own terms, a life lived mostly in his imagination. Glenn Gould followed his own advice.

Baby Glenn with his mother, Florence Gould, in 1932

A Welcome Addition

Glenn Herbert Gould was born on September 25, 1932, three years after the start of the Great Depression. In those days, most babies were delivered at home. Glenn was too.

Like many exceptional people, he was an only child. His parents, Florence and Russell Herbert (Bert) Gould, had tried to have children before. Unfortunately, Mrs. Gould had lost several babies. She was forty-two years of age when Glenn arrived. The Goulds were delighted.

Mrs. Gould had decided long before Glenn was born that if she had a son, his name would be Glenn.

His mother would play a very important role in Glenn's life. Except for his cousin Jessie Greig, Florence Gould was really the only woman with whom Glenn was very close throughout his life.

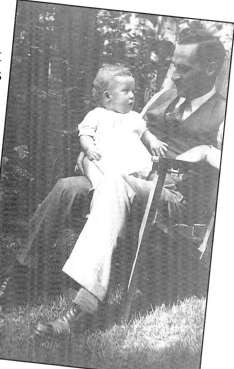

Glenn with his father Bert in 1933

Mrs. Gould was an exceptionally talented musician. Glenn was very lucky to have someone so gifted and knowledgeable as his first teacher.

Several million reed organs were built in North America between 1850 and 1950. Most had one keyboard, although some had up to three. They usually had two pedals and two or two and a half sets of metal reeds. The player would pump the pedals to force air past the reeds.

A Musical Family

Glenn arrived into a musical household. His earliest musical influences were right in his own home. Even before he was born, Glenn was surrounded by music. His mother played music the entire time she was pregnant with Glenn.

Both his parents were good singers. Mr. Gould had played the violin until he damaged his hand and had to stop. Mrs. Gould was a music teacher, a talented pianist and a singing coach. Glenn's Uncle Bruce played trumpet, and his grandmother, Mary, was a pianist. Even before Glenn was a year old, his grandmother held him on her lap while she played the piano and he hummed. His grandmother also played the organ and kept stacks of anthems by Victorian composers piled on her reed organ, whose pedals she pumped vigorously. Glenn could also claim to have a very famous musician in his family tree—the composer Edvard Grieg, who was a distant relative of his mother.

Early Signs

Robert Fulford and Glenn met in elementary school and formed a strong friendship that lasted through high school and into adulthood. At one point, they formed a small company called New Music Associates. They produced three well-attended concerts at the Toronto Conservatory of Music, which later became the Royal Conservatory of Music. Glenn was the main attraction at each one. At one of these concerts, he played J. S. Bach's *Goldberg Variations*, music that would soon bring him great fame.

Robert Fulford went on to become one of Canada's most respected writers and music critics. His work has appeared in many major magazines and newspapers.

No parent could possibly be prepared for a child like Glenn, although many parents wish that their children be exceptional. Mr. and Mrs. Gould couldn't have known just how special their son would prove to be. But they soon began to learn, as did everyone else. Glenn was spectacularly gifted. His boyhood friend Robert Fulford wrote many years later that Glenn's arrival into the Gould household was "like having a mountain range appear suddenly in the backyard."

Like that most famous of child prodigies, Mozart, Glenn showed early signs of musical genius. Mr. Gould often told people that his son would wave his hands like a conductor when he was just a few days old, and that he would hum when he was hungry. His father also said that even as a baby Glenn never pounded on the keys of the piano as most children do. Instead, he pressed them down gently. Maybe his father was exaggerating a little bit. After all, he was very proud of his son.

Nevertheless, by the age of three, Glenn, who was left-handed, showed remarkable ability in music. He could read music before he could read words. He could name piano notes just by hearing them. Before he started school, he was already making up his own tunes at the piano. When he was five, Glenn told his father that he would be a concert pianist.

This was Glenn's home until he was in his late twenties, when he moved into his own apartment on St. Clair Avenue in Toronto. He continued to live in the city for the rest of his life, except for those times when he was touring or when he retreated to the cottage at Uptergrove on Lake Simcoe. Many years later he would make a documentary about his city, *Glenn Gould's Toronto*.

A Comfortable Life

The Gould family lived in a modest house that stood on a tree-lined street near Lake Ontario in Toronto's Beach area, a quiet, pretty place that would soon be known as the home of one of Canada's musical geniuses. Bert Gould's furrier business, which he'd inherited from his father Thomas, earned more than enough money to allow the family a comfortable lifestyle.

Even during the Depression, a time when millions of North Americans were unemployed, his parents never had to worry about money. They were very supportive of Glenn, and money for music lessons was always available. The Goulds spent approximately three thousand dollars each year on his music education. In the 1940s, that was quite a lot of money. Bert also built an addition to the house so Glenn could practice any time he wanted.

They loved their gifted son dearly, but they didn't spoil him. They tried their best to give him a normal life.

The Goulds were among the lucky people who were not affected much during the period of the Great Depression, which lasted from 1929 until the 1940s. It was a time of great economic hardship for people in Canada and many other industrialized nations. There was a severe increase in unemployment, many businesses and even banks went bankrupt, and millions of people lost their jobs, homes and savings.

A prodigy is someone with exceptional talent that shows itself very early. There have been many child musical prodigies. Mozart is perhaps the most famous one. Niccolo Paganini, a violinist, astounded people with his skill. Lord Yehudi Menuhin was another famous prodigy. A violinist of extraordinary ability, he knew and admired Glenn very much. Sir Ernest MacMillan, conductor of the Toronto Symphony Orchestra, was also a prodigy, although, like Glenn, he denied it.

Raising Glenn

Mr. and Mrs. Gould had definite ideas about how their young genius should be raised. Still, it couldn't have been easy for them at times. Glenn was a slight boy, and Florence tended to worry about his eating habits and his health. Glenn may not have been strong physically, but he could be stubborn. He avoided exercise, and he was a real sloucher who liked to slump when he sat.

Although Glenn's parents were very proud of him, they probably also felt a little overwhelmed by their son at times. Glenn was smart and curious, and he seemed to know a lot about many things.

Music, of course, was central in his upbringing. In addition to encouraging his piano studies, and later the organ, Glenn's parents made every effort to make sure he heard good music, and there was plenty of it in Toronto at the time.

His parents refused to call him a prodigy. Of course, he was one, and they knew it, but they understood the risks faced by child prodigies. They knew that some parents of talented children push them into performing before they are mature enough to handle the pressures of the stage or the praise heaped upon them by an adoring public who view them as curiosities.

Glenn playing the organ

So the Goulds did their best to protect Glenn from such a life. They would never allow him to be exploited, and that meant he would not perform in public until he was ready. But a normal life would be impossible. He was too talented. Years later, as an adult, he always denied that he'd been a child prodigy. But the undeniable fact is that he was.

Although Glenn's parents didn't want him to perform in public at a young age, they soon realized they couldn't hide such a talented boy for long. Being devout people, they let Glenn play at various church socials, where he was a great success. His first public performance took place at the Uxbridge United Church in 1937, when he was about five years old.

Glenn playing the piano at home with his dog

I am Not a Prodigy

Even prodigies sometimes have bad days. Glenn had only one job in his lifetime, and it didn't last very long. Actually, it wasn't really even a job. While he was still a boy, he was asked to play organ for the services at an Anglican Church. But he was dismissed from this position because he couldn't concentrate and kept losing his place in the music when the congregation sang.

At seven, Glenn received the highest marks in Ontario for the Grade Four Piano Examination. By the age of ten, he had mastered Book One of J.S. Bach's *Well-Tempered Clavier*, and only two years later, he completed all the examinations up to Grade Ten in piano and organ up to Grade Eight. Shortly after, he earned his Associate Diploma from the Conservatory with the highest grade in the entire country. At thirteen, he was the youngest musician ever to have achieved this difficult goal. All of this was followed by one success after another. The same year, he took part in his first radio broadcast and won the Kiwanis Music Festival's Gordon V. Thompson scholarship.

Glenn received first class honours on his Grade III and IV piano exam

A Mind of His Own

Although Glenn didn't like sports, when he was older, he loved to drive big, fast cars. Unfortunately, he was a terrible driver. People were afraid to ride with him because he talked non-stop and waved his arms around, often failing to look at the road. Sometimes he banged up his cars. Once, he hit a truck. And he was known to hit the concrete pillars in the parking garage at his apartment from time to time. He also was well known to the police for speeding and received many tickets.

When Glenn told the graduating class in 1964 not to pay too much attention to the advice of others, he was speaking from experience.

Glenn knew his own mind from the start. Most children care what their peers think of them and try hard to be part of a group. Not Glenn. He refused to play sports, even marbles. Deep down, he may have wanted to, but even as a child, he was wary about hurting his hands. Often, he'd stuff them into his pockets and stand by himself while others played. He also disliked competitions and contests of any sort, even though he hated to lose at chess and croquet.

Many kids love to swear, sometimes just to shock adults. Glenn hated swearing. His parents didn't tolerate foul language, and neither did Glenn. In fact, when he was a grown-up, vulgar language made him uncomfortable.

After listening to a recording by one of the world's greatest opera singers, Enrico Caruso, Glenn convinced a friend that the famous Italian singer was really not very good.

Glenn with his dog Nick

Like his parents, Glenn was an honest man. He had no fear about stating what he believed. All his life he challenged what others thought of music and how it should be played. Sometimes he annoyed critics, conductors, musicians and audiences. Often it was hard to tell whether Glenn was serious or whether he was exaggerating to make a point. For example, he once said he could teach anyone the mechanics of playing the piano in an hour. Was he being serious or was he kidding to make a point?

Glenn also developed strong opinions about famous composers. For example, he didn't care much for the music of Frédéric Chopin or Franz Liszt, two composers admired by many musicians and listeners. Nor was he overly fond of much of Mozart's music, even though he played it beautifully. He also disliked Italian opera.

Glenn was highly intelligent, and he had a quirky sense of humour, so sometimes it was difficult to know whether he was just making comments to get a reaction, or if he really meant them.

Glenn's Mentor

Mrs. Gould was a loving mother who believed in discipline, but she was also much more. She was his mentor, someone who recognized his genius and guided him through the early years, and even after.

Devoted to Glenn, she made many sacrifices of her own time to help her brilliant son. She nurtured his musical development from the start and was his only teacher until he was ten years of age. From the beginning, when he was only three years old, she encouraged him to sing the notes as he played them. Maybe that's why later on he could hear music in his mind. She was always home when he practised and corrected him immediately if he made a mistake. After he'd practiced for many hours, he would rest his head on her lap, and she'd pat it. Glenn needed lots of love and affection and got it from both his parents. Perhaps that is one reason why he grew up to be a very gentle human being.

Florence Gould's niece, Jessie Greig, believed that her aunt hoped from the very beginning that Glenn would one day be a classical pianist. Florence predicted that one day Glenn would have "the world at his feet."

Meddlin' Country Cuz

Edvard Grieg: a famous Norwegian composer best known for his *Peer Gynt Suite*. Despite the difference in the spelling of the name, Jessie's family was distantly related to the composer.

Jessie Greig was five years older than Glenn. At eighteen, she came to stay with the Goulds for a year while she attended teacher's college in Toronto. The two immediately became fast friends, although Glenn was a bit jealous at first, probably because he thought he wouldn't be the centre of attention. But he got over that quickly. The two had great fun arguing. Glenn loved to tease her and used to call her his "meddlin'-country-cuzin". He remained very close to Jessie his entire life. Often they'd speak almost daily on the telephone, Glenn's favourite method of communication with friends and acquaintances. Glenn talked with Jessie about science, philosophy, world affairs, education and his many projects.

Elementary Schooldays

Glenn is in the back row of this class portrait at Williamson Road Public School. In Glenn's day, students in elementary school received percentages out of one hundred for each course rather than letter grades. The percentages were added and divided by the number of courses. Then the student would receive a final percentage for the term or year's work. Students who received at least 50% went on to the next grade. Those who didn't repeated the grade.

Glenn attended Williamson Road Public School, which was just a short distance from his home. Every morning he would trudge to the three-storey building to face another day of boredom. Some days, school can be boring for most students. For Glenn, elementary school was deadly dull most of the time. Like many students, he probably spent a lot of time staring at the clock, watching the seconds tick by.

He made few friends. Glenn refused to catch a ball or play any kind of sport because he didn't want to hurt his hands. During recess, he often stood by himself while the other children played. He also had the habit of conducting an imaginary orchestra as he walked home from school. The other students found his behaviour very odd. He once said, "I found going to school a most unhappy experience and got along miserably with most of my teachers and all of my fellow students."

Like many kids, Glenn loved to learn, but he disliked school. Maybe if there had been programs for gifted students in those days, he might have enjoyed elementary school more. However, he did tell Jessie many years later that there were at least two teachers in his school career whom he liked and who had challenged him.

A New Teacher

Alberto Guerrero teaching Glenn

Florence knew that someday she would no longer be able to teach her son. When Glenn was ten and still at Williamson Road Public School, she decided he needed a piano teacher who could prepare him for the difficult examinations at the Toronto Conservatory of Music. Glenn wanted to complete his associate degree in performance, and this would require a teacher with exceptional skills. She asked Alberto Guerrero if he would teach her son. Guerrero was a talented concert pianist originally from Chile. He agreed, and for almost ten years he guided Glenn.

Guerrero influenced Glenn in many ways. He taught him to sit lower at the piano keyboard. He also showed him how to play with flatter fingers. He and Glenn spent many hours talking and arguing about music and its interpretations. Glenn was very headstrong and believed he was always right. The new teacher was patient with his talented student. Guerrero realized immediately that the way to teach Glenn was to let him discover things for himself.

With his thinning hair, glasses and gentle manner, Guerrero was like a kind uncle who

Glenn's new teacher was a highly accomplished musician. He had founded and conducted the first symphony orchestra in Santiago, Chile. He had also given premiere performances of music by Debussy and Ravel. When he moved to Toronto, he introduced that city's audiences to the piano compositions of modern composers like Schoenberg, Stravinsky, Milhaud and Hindemith. Glenn liked the music of Schoenberg and admired the composer.

let the boy explore the world of music. The two would also play croquet together. Even though Glenn always said he hated competition, he played fiercely and hated to lose.

Guerrero didn't like Glenn's many mannerisms at the keyboard. He tried to convince Glenn to sit still and to stop singing and humming while he played, but he had no luck.

Glenn and Guerrero playing croquet

A Second Home

Like many Torontonians, the Goulds owned a cottage. The family spent their summers at Uptergrove on Lake Simcoe. This retreat was very important to Glenn for much of his life. For a young boy, life at the cottage was perfect. Glenn and his English setter Nick spent hours on the lake in his cedar motor boat. He strolled through the maple and birch trees with his dog, conducting the music he heard in his mind. He played the family's Chickering piano to his heart's content.

The family cottage at Lake Simcoe

Glenn loved the sound and the touch of this old piano. Some evenings he gave performances for his parents and their friends. He even formed a little group with two cottage pals. The three boys would put on shows, and Glenn would sometimes try to record their music.

The small, white cottage was a sanctuary. He hated to go back to the city. When it was time to go back to school in September, he would become very sad. The cottage was his haven, a place of peace where he could just be himself. Of course, life at the cottage was about more than just music.

A Fishing Story

Glenn's first boat was a fifteen-foot cedar skiff. It had an electric motor and two twelve-volt storage batteries.

Many people fondly remember going fishing for the first time. Glenn remembered too, but not fondly.

When Glenn was six, he went fishing with a neighbour. Glenn caught a fish, and the experience upset him badly. Years later, he told a reporter how he felt that day. "We went out in the boat, and I was the first to catch a fish. And when the little perch came up and started wiggling about, I suddenly saw this thing entirely from the fish's point of view— it was such a powerful experience. I picked up the fish and said I was going to throw it back."

But the neighbour pushed him back in his seat and grabbed the fish. Glenn screamed in anger. Later, he realized he'd probably been rocking the boat while shouting about the poor fish. When he returned home, he tried to persuade his father to give up fishing. Glenn's father was an avid angler, but Glenn hounded his father for years until he gave in and quit.

Glenn never outgrew his dislike of fishing and became a great champion of fish. Every summer he sped around Lake Simcoe in his boat, racing close to anglers on their boats, spooking the fish. The anglers were not pleased. They shouted at Glenn, but he just shouted right back at them. The next day he would do it all over again.

A Watery Orchestra

If Glenn were alive today, he would be very upset to know that his beloved lake attracts more anglers each year than any other inland lake in Ontario. They catch thousands of perch, pike, bass, pickerel and lake trout.

Lake Simcoe is a very large lake. With a surface area of 725 square kilometres, it's the largest body of fresh water in Ontario, except for the Great Lakes. Though beautiful, Lake Simcoe can also be dangerous for boaters. A strong, steady breeze can make the water quite choppy.

One of Glenn's boating expeditions almost ended in disaster. One day he was out on the lake, probably looking for anglers to annoy, when a storm blew up. Afraid his determined son might be in trouble, Mr. Gould went out in another boat, only to find Glenn in his boat waving his arms, conducting the waves. Walking home from school wasn't the only place Glenn conducted the orchestra he heard in his mind.

The Accident

Life at the cottage was fun, but one had to be careful, too. When Glenn was about ten, he and couple of pals were lugging Glenn's cedar boat up a rail Bert had built to make the job of hauling the boat out of the water and up the beach easier.

Glenn stood on the rail, tugging at the boat. Suddenly he slipped and fell straight down, landing on some rocks. It wasn't a long drop, but he hurt his back. For some time after the accident, his parents took him to see several doctors because the pain didn't go away. They found no real damage.

When he was older, Glenn often complained of pain in his hands, shoulders, neck and back. Maybe that early accident affected him somehow. No one really knows for sure, but all his life he tried to figure out why he would have pain in those places.

Health Woes

The card said:

Your cooperation will be appreciated…

A pianist's hands are sometimes injured in ways which cannot be predicted.

Needless to say, this could be quite serious.

Therefore, I will very much appreciate it if handshaking can be avoided.

This will eliminate embarrassment all around. Rest assured that there is no intent to be discourteous—the aim is to prevent any possibility of injury.

Thank you.
GLENN GOULD

When her son was a child, Mrs. Gould sometimes thought that Glenn looked sickly. She worried about his health. As he grew older, he became very health conscious. He feared catching a cold or the flu. Even in summer he would wear a coat, scarf, gloves and cap. He also avoided physical contact with other people.

He was becoming even more protective of his hands. Most pianists are, because they depend on their hands for their living. Glenn was no different in this. When he started to become famous, he insured his hands for $100,000. He also took a most unusual step. To keep from shaking hands with people after a performance, he had a card printed which he gave out to people after concerts.

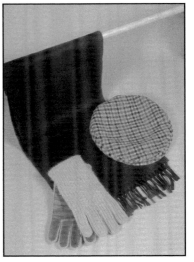

Glenn's hat, gloves and scarf are in the collections of the National Library of Canada

So Many Other Talents

Glenn's paper was called *The Daily Woof: The Animal Paper.* In it he would describe his pets and the things that happened to them. One story in *The Daily Woof* was about a squirrel.

SQUIRREL ATTRACTS ATTENTION
A black squirrel attracted much attention here yesterday P.M. when he dragged a large chunk of bread across the street spreading crumbs on the lawn. He is wanted for questioning by local authorities in other recent thefts.

Glenn was very curious. His parents were probably a bit awed by Glenn's ability to absorb information. He was fascinated by recording technology and spent hours listening to the radio. He loved words and reading. When he was very young, he wrote his own newspaper. Throughout his entire life, Glenn loved to write. He once said that if he were not a musician, he would have been a writer. Although he always planned to write a novel, he never did.

Glenn also showed early promise as a composer. When he was about five, he started to make up his own tunes.

A copy of a musical piece composed by Glenn called "Five Short Pieces"

Animal Rights

Like most children, Glenn loved animals. He had many pets and gave them unusual names. He called his goldfish Bach, Beethoven, Chopin and Haydn, after the composers. He had a bird named Mozart. His dogs had unusual names, too: Sinbad, Sir Nickolson of Garelocheed and Banquo, a character from Shakespeare's play *Macbeth.* At various times he also owned rabbits and turtles.

He befriended a skunk that scavenged for garbage at the cottage. The skunk was trapped, and Mr. Gould told Glenn to do whatever he wanted with it. Soon the little skunk was eating out of Glenn's hand. The creature became a pet, and Glenn wrote a song in its honour.

Glenn's respect and affection for animals was an important part of his personality. He could not tolerate even the idea of cruelty toward them. He believed that people did not have the right to kill animals to suit their own purposes. For that reason he found it difficult to accept that his father was a furrier, because furriers make coats out of animal skin.

Years later, Glenn was asked to compose the music for *The Wars,* a film based on Timothy Findley's book of the same name. One of the scenes has a dead horse in it. Glenn became very upset. He needed to be reassured that the animal had not been killed for use in the scene. He said simply that he could not work on the film if it had been.

Once, a friend told him that a famous musician had told a joke that had something to do with cruelty to animals. Glenn refused to have anything to do with the musician. In his quiet, gentle way, Glenn was an animal rights activist long before the protection of animals became an important movement.

Lyrics from Glenn's skunk song:
"I am a skunk, a skunk am I, skunking is all I know, I want no more, I am a skunk, a skunk I'll remain."

Glenn sang a lot, especially when he played. In one scene of the documentary *Glenn Gould's Toronto*, he mentions that he had once sung to cows in a field. So on film, he goes to the Toronto Zoo and serenades elephants with his rendition of music by Gustav Mahler.

The Boy Makes his Mark

The Kiwanis Music Festival was founded in 1944 by Sir Ernest MacMillan, who was a well-known Canadian composer, organist, pianist and conductor. Each year, thousands of students compete in the festival on all kinds of instruments, including voice.

Mr. and Mrs. Gould realized that Glenn's talent couldn't remain hidden any longer. The performances at various church socials were fine. They made people aware of his talent, but sooner or later he would have to play in a more formal setting, as all aspiring young musicians do.

When Glenn was twelve, he competed in the first annual Kiwanis Music Festival and won first prize in the piano trophy competition. Hundreds of students had entered, including senior students from the Toronto Conservatory of Music. Several of the competitors were very skilled musicians who later enjoyed successful careers as performers.

On that day, Glenn walked onto the stage wearing short pants, sat down and played. From the first note, he captivated the large audience. When the last note faded away, people applauded wildly. Not yet in his teens, Glenn was becoming known for his exceptional musicianship.

Glenn's hand on the organ

Now it was time for a formal recital. He gave his first one on December 12, 1945. Glenn played the organ, not the piano. His public debut on that difficult instrument was very impressive. The recital was sponsored by the Casavant Society, named after Casavant Frères, Canada's most respected builder of organs. Glenn's pal Robert Fulford sat beside him on the bench and turned the pages of the music.

Glenn chose music by Johann Sebastian Bach, Albert Dupuis and Felix Mendelssohn. He was only thirteen, but he played confidently. One critic commented that Glenn "played the organ last evening as many a full-grown concert organist couldn't if he tried. A genius he is...and in every detail his playing had the fearless authority and finesse of a master."

Glenn on Competitions

Glenn attended Montreal's First International Violin Competition as an observer. Afterwards, he wrote an essay, "We Who Are About to be Disqualified Salute You." In it he suggested that it's not the most creative or original musician who usually wins.

When he was much older, Glenn had a few things to say about music competitions. For a man who liked to drive fast cars and who detested losing at croquet or chess as a boy, he was most definitely against competition in music.

He had competed in the Kiwanis Music Festival and won, and he had gone through the Conservatory with top marks, but he believed that grading or evaluating music students led to a competitive atmosphere, and he questioned the value of it.

He developed this idea slowly over time. Later, he argued that the entire business of performing in public made him feel demeaned. Much to everyone's surprise, he suggested that one creative way of opting out was to concentrate on recording music.

Standing his Ground

Because he was different, Glenn was often teased. Sometimes he came home in tears. One day as Glenn walked home from school, the worst bully at Williamson Road Public School tried to punch him. That was a big mistake. Even though Glenn was not particularly strong or athletic, he was brave.

Williamson Road Public School

Glenn hit the bully really hard. The other boy was stunned. Glenn didn't give him time to think. He grabbed the bully by his lapels, shook him and said, "If you ever come near me again, I will kill you." Glenn was extremely angry. He probably scared himself as much as he frightened the bully.

That was the only time Glenn ever hit anyone. No one even remembers him really losing his temper. Glenn hated violence. He thought violence was stupid and inhuman, but on that day, he'd had enough and stood his ground.

Life in High School

Glenn's ability with numbers proved very useful when he was older. He played the stock market. When he died, his estate was worth about $750,000. Glenn earned much of this money on the stock market, managing to invest in good stocks even when the market was doing poorly.

After he completed elementary school, Glenn went to Malvern Collegiate. Life was easier there than it had been at Williamson, although he still didn't like school. He was allowed to take a special program. He attended classes in the mornings; afternoons he spent studying music and practising.

He kept to himself in high school as well, but he wasn't teased as he had been in elementary school. He also made a few friends. The other students thought he was peculiar, but they respected his talent and his intelligence.

Glenn had his favourite subjects, and he worked very hard on these. Like many great musicians, he excelled at mathematics, especially geometry. He whizzed through Grade Ten geometry in just two months. History fascinated him, especially tales about explorers. He loved English literature and writing, although his teachers thought he composed sentences that were too long and windy. His penmanship and spelling remained as terrible as they had been in elementary school.

At Malvern, Glenn also got the chance to show off his skill as a composer. He wrote his first serious piece, a piano sonata, when he was fifteen. He also composed and performed music for the drama club's production of *Twelfth Night*, a play by William Shakespeare.

Glenn didn't like to talk about his technique. If people asked him about playing the piano, he would remind them of the story of the centipede who was asked by a toad how she managed to control so many legs. The centipede started to think about it and found she couldn't walk.

The Centipede was happy, quite
Until the Toad in fun
Said, "Pray which leg goes after which
When you begin to run?"
That worked her mind to such a pitch,
She lay distracted in a ditch
Considering how to run.
            -Anonymous Fable

An Exceptional Ear and Fabulous Technique

Everyone who got to know Glenn soon learned that he had highly unusual abilities. He'd been born with absolute pitch, sometimes called perfect pitch. A person with absolute pitch can name notes upon hearing them as easily and accurately as most people can name colours upon seeing them. Mozart, for example, could identify a note made by a bell or a chiming pocket watch. Absolute pitch is a very rare gift. Only about one in ten thousand North Americans has perfect pitch. Glenn believed that if the gift of absolute pitch were taken away from him, he wouldn't be able to function.

Glenn was also extremely sensitive to the quality of sound. He spent most of his life looking for the perfect piano, one which sounded like the one he heard in his mind.

Glenn's exceptional hearing was matched by his superior control of his hands. He could play the most complicated passages with ease, making each note distinct. This was all the more amazing because he claimed that he never really had to practise new pieces very hard.

1946: A Major Break

The Toronto Symphony Orchestra was founded in 1922 and gave its first performance in 1923. The TSO was to Glenn as a home baseball team is to sports fans. He loved the orchestra and never said an unkind word about it.

Artur Schnabel (1882-1951) was an Austrian pianist known for his interpretations of Ludwig van Beethoven's music.

The first year after the end of World War II, 1946, when Glenn was fourteen, proved to be a very important one. This boy, who had already distinguished himself from thousands of pianists in Ontario, received a most flattering invitation and also really annoyed his teacher.

The Toronto Symphony Orchestra asked Glenn to play the first concert in their Secondary School Series. Alberto Guerrero suggested he play the Piano Concerto No. 4 in G Major by Ludwig van Beethoven.

In preparation, the young high school student performed the first movement of this music with the Toronto Conservatory Symphony Orchestra on May 8, 1946, at Massey Hall. On that occasion, his famous stubbornness showed itself clearly.

He loved the piano playing of Artur Schnabel and had listened to the master's recording of the G Major Concerto many, many times. He played along with parts of Schnabel's Beethoven recording, imitating the master.

Guerrero was not happy about this. The teacher wanted his pupil to put the records away and learn to play the piece at a slightly faster tempo. Glenn did as Guerrero wanted.

Glenn sometimes embellished events. His memory of the review was different from the reporter's actual words, which were: "Glenn Gould's offering was the opening movement of the Beethoven G Major Piano Concerto. Not too much dynamic range here, phrasing a little choppy and sometimes puzzling to one familiar with Schnabel, but with obvious possibilities."

Glenn had a good trial run with this concerto. The next year, 1947, he made his debut with the Toronto Symphony Orchestra and played the entire concerto to very favourable reviews.

After weeks of preparation, the night of the performance arrived. Glenn strode onto the stage, sat down, and played the concerto the way he wanted to, ignoring what his teacher had told him.

Years later, he wrote a short essay about that performance. In it, he said, "I left in high spirits, my teacher was shattered, and the press, on the whole, was quite kind." Glenn also wrote that one of the critics at the end of his review had asked, "Who does the kid think he is, Schnabel?"

This period was important to Glenn's development. He had to discover for himself whether he had the ability to be a serious concert artist. He was getting ready in his own way and in his own time.

Humming and Swaying

Whenever musicians talk about musical geniuses, the name Wolfgang Amadeus Mozart inevitably comes up. By the age of five, he was composing his own music. By thirteen he had mastered the harpsichord, violin and organ. He began his concert career early, touring Europe, astounding everyone who heard him play.

Alberto Guerrero wasn't the only one who grimaced at Glenn's weird behaviour at the keyboard. Almost from the beginning of his concert career, critics referred to Glenn's odd mannerisms at the piano. When he played, he hummed, sang and conducted with his free hand. Sometimes he would sit with his legs crossed.

Some music critics were merciless in their comments. After a concert in Detroit, Michigan, one wrote: "Seldom has a more exquisite performance been heard...or a worse one witnessed." Another was just as cruel: "In his current phase of development it is his tragedy that his behaviour at the piano produced laughter in his audience..."

Glenn hated being criticized for anything, and he was hurt by such comments, but he could not change the way he played. Most people eventually just accepted his odd habits at the keyboard and ignored them, concentrating instead on the beauty of his playing.

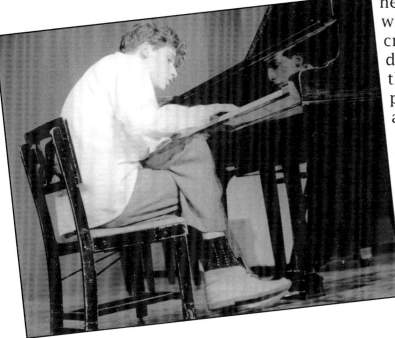

World War II was a global conflict that was probably the most devastating war in the history of humankind. It started in 1939, when Glenn was just seven years old, and lasted until 1945.

Millions of people, soldiers and civilians, died. Others lost their homes and became refugees. Many of them came to Canada after the war, hoping for a new life free of the terrible hardship they had endured. The war formed a backdrop to everyone's life. People in Toronto became used to ration cards for food, posters announcing Victory War Bonds to raise money for the war effort and female streetcar drivers (because so many men were off fighting in the war).

Good Years

The years immediately after the war were very good for Glenn. He was developing a reputation as a wonderful musician. He had one success after another.

In 1947, he gave his first public solo recital on piano in Eaton Auditorium. The next year he composed his first major composition, a piano sonata. Two years later he wrote his Sonata for Bassoon and Piano, performed in his first major concert outside of his hometown and made his debut on CBC Radio.

Glenn was just four years old when the Canadian Broadcasting Corporation was launched in 1936, but he soon became one of its most devoted listeners. Today in the age of TV and computer, it's hard to imagine just how important radio was. In Canada, CBC Radio formed a vital link for people across the nation. They relied on the corporation for current events, music and drama. The CBC played a very significant role in Glenn's musical development and career. When he was older, the network gave him a chance to perform, write scripts and make documentaries. It also brought Glenn's music-making into the homes of thousands of Canadians.

He must have been very pleased, but he was also growing discontented, and when Glenn was unhappy, change was sure to follow. Soon, he would take control of his life and destiny.

Difficult Decisions

Glenn's later comment about Guerrero was puzzling. He probably didn't mean that he hadn't learned anything from him. It was simply Glenn's way of saying that he had really started to study on his own in earnest, without anyone else's guidance.

Nearing the end of his teen years, Glenn made two major decisions. He had had enough of book learning, so he quit Malvern Collegiate before graduating. Naturally, his parents were not pleased.

The second decision was perhaps the harder of the two and took a bit more time. Every student must at some time leave his teacher behind and go out on his own. Every good teacher knows this and prepares the student for that day. Glenn, however, decided on his own that he'd had enough of piano studies with Alberto Guerrero.

His teacher had always been patient and kind with his star pupil. Over the years, they had become friends. But Glenn believed he had outgrown his old teacher. His parents disagreed. So did Alberto Guerrero. Glenn got really frustrated with all of them. Sometimes, when he would talk to Jessie about it, he would have tears in his eyes.

No matter what anyone said, Glenn refused to budge. He'd made up his mind. In 1952, at the age of twenty, he left his teacher. His parents gave him their support, but Guerrero must have been very hurt.

Later in life, Glenn considered himself to be mostly self-taught, claiming that he began his serious study of music after he parted ways with his old teacher.

What Now?

Glenn would have to compete for attention with many other talented pianists. Much older musicians like Vladimir Horowitz and Arthur Rubinstein had set the musical bar very high. As well, there were other young players out there who were Glenn's contemporaries and who would soon become well known: Leon Fleisher, Van Cliburn, Lorin Hollander, Gary Graffman and Seymour Lipkin, to name just a few.

Just twenty years old, Glenn was on his own. This was a very serious situation. The world of concert performance is highly competitive. People who aspire to the world stage must be absolutely prepared. Although he was respected in Canada, Glenn was not well known anywhere else. The world had yet to hear about him, and there were many good pianists out there.

Perhaps he was a little worried, but he was also determined and confident in his abilities. Great things lay ahead for him. Soon he would astound people all over the world with his playing. First, though, he had to prepare himself. He would be his own teacher and critic.

Artur Rubenstein

Vladimir Horowitz

Glenn playing his Chickering piano at the cottage

Glenn had a phenomenal memory and could memorize musical scores simply by reading them. Guerrero had encouraged him to do this, because on one occasion Glenn had forgotten the music during a recital. This unnerved him. His teacher then showed him how to study music away from the keyboard.

Taking A Risk

Glenn was courageous. He was always prepared to take a chance with music and in life. So he removed himself from Toronto's music scene for a while and went to the cottage, leaving only to perform concerts arranged for him by Walter Homburger, his agent.

Life at the cottage turned into a comfortable routine. Music now absorbed him completely. He didn't have to worry about school, or about preparing lessons for Guerrero or anyone else. All that was behind him now.

He spent hours practising. He'd play a few bars, then stop, walk around the room, gaze out the window thinking, hearing the music in his mind over and over and over again. Sometimes he'd sing what he was hearing, then sit down and play again. He'd repeat this many, many times each day and night. He was searching for the best way to express the music. He was struggling for perfection.

When he wasn't at the piano or studying musical scores, he walked with his dog, hearing music in his mind, unaware of anything or anyone else.

Locals in the village were used to this absent-minded young man. Whenever the store owner in Uptergrove found crumpled dollar bills in the snow, he assumed they were Glenn's and saved them for him.

His Reputation Grows

In Calgary, a reporter from *The Albertan* asked Mrs. Gould if she had any advice to give other mothers who had musical children. Florence Gould said that they would have to give up a lot of time and social activities. She also added that Glenn, even though he was nineteen, didn't have time for girls, and that she was happy he didn't at this point in his life.

Florence Gould probably didn't suspect at the time that Glenn would never really have time for dating. Yet, even though he was a shy man in many ways, he made many friends, and some of them were women. He never married. His cousin Jessie once remarked that it would have been hard for a woman to be married to Glenn, because he was really married to his music.

By the time Glenn retreated to the cottage, he had already impressed audiences in Toronto and caught the attention of that city's musical elite. He'd also given his first major concert outside Toronto, at the University of Western Ontario. Shortly after, he had his debut on the CBC radio network.

Glenn's agent, Walter Homburger, had also arranged several concerts in major Canadian cities. The first was in Vancouver. Florence went with him. He so impressed the audience that he received five curtain calls. Then he went to Calgary, where he gave a recital for the Calgary Women's Musical Club. The following year, 1952, the same year he left Guererro and went to the cottage, he performed on CBC-TV. This was a landmark because Glenn was the first pianist to be televised in performance in Canada.

During his period of solitude and searching, Glenn learned a great deal about music and about himself. Yet every musician has to keep performing, because the public easily forgets, and Glenn had to do the same.

The young Canadian pianist was a success everywhere he played. In 1953, he appeared for the first time at the Stratford Festival.

Many years later, Glenn's boyhood friend Robert Fulford wrote that even when he was very young, Glenn was isolated because he was already trying hard to become great. He knew he was special, and he knew what he wanted to be.

Then he gave his first recital in eastern Canada in St. John, New Brunswick. It was time, too, to astound francophone audiences. After his debut concert with the Montreal Symphony on December 14, 1954, the *Montreal Star* called him "one of the greatest musical personalities of this generation."

The more Glenn played, the more other musicians heard about this young Canadian wizard of the keyboard. His reputation in Canada grew steadily. However, if he was to become known internationally, he would have to impress audiences south of the border.

Glenn discovered a new way to learn complex music. One day, while he was practising, a maid turned on a vacuum cleaner. Suddenly, Glenn couldn't hear the piano, but he could really concentrate on the movement of his fingers, the feel of the keyboard, and the music as he heard it in his mind's ear. The problem he was having with the piece cleared up. After that he sometimes turned on one or two radios at full volume while learning a particularly difficult passage.

American Debuts

After the concert, a *Washington Post* reporter wrote, "...it is unlikely that the year 1955 will bring us a finer piano recital than that played yesterday in the Phillips Gallery. We shall be lucky if it brings us others of equal beauty and significance."

Then as now, musicians went to the United States to establish a major career in music. Glenn was twenty-two years of age, a young man with some experience and a solid reputation in Canada. Was he ready to go south of the border and compete for attention with all the other brilliant pianists?

Glenn had two American debuts. The first took place on January 2, 1955, at the Phillips Gallery in Washington, D.C., the capital of the United States. Glenn showed his courage by taking a huge risk with the pieces he chose to perform. Unlike many young pianists who choose pieces from the traditional repertoire for their debut, Glenn picked difficult music by J. S. Bach, Alban Berg and Anton Webern among others.

He was taking a huge chance—again. If he played less than his very best, the critics would be merciless. His gamble paid off. He played beautifully. Now, the biggest challenge of his budding music career lay ahead.

The Great Trial: January 11, 1955

Every musician dreams of playing in New York. The Big Apple's audiences were as sophisticated and critical then as they are today. New Yorkers could hear the world's greatest musicians and singers any day of the week.

Glenn called New York "Debutown," and for his second American debut, he rented Town Hall in New York and paid for his own advertising. Only about 200 people attended, not a huge number. However, one very important man sat in the hall that night: David Oppenheim of Columbia Records. A distinguished-looking man with grey hair, Oppenheim was highly respected in the music world. He was about to play a very important role in Glenn's life.

So the pressure was on. Expectations were high. Glenn had much to live up to. With a successful debut in Washington and high praise in a very important newspaper, he had to be at his best.

GLENN GOULD

"It seems almost patronizing impertinence to praise his playing in conventional terms."
Ottawa Journal, Feb. '53

"Mr. Gould has a rare gift for lifting notes off paper and making you forget that they ever existed as mere symbols in dry ink."
CBC—Nov. '53

CANADIAN PIANIST

"A marvellous recital, a great revelation; take good note of his name, you will hear it much talked about in the future."
Montreal Le Canada, Nov. '52

Town Hall, Tues. Jan. 11th, 8.30 p.m.
TICKETS: $2.30, 1.73, 1.15. Loges seating six: $17.28 (All tax incl.)
Program: Fantasia for Organ-Sweelinck; 5 Sinfonias and Partita No. 5 in G Major-Bach; Sonata in E Major, Op. 109-Beethoven; Sonata Opus 1-Berg; Variations-Webern.

The evening was tense and exciting. Glenn was probably quite anxious while he waited in the wings, although he said later that he wasn't. Nervous or not, he strode onto the stage, one hand in his pocket. Instead of the traditional tuxedo, he wore a dark business suit.

Some people thought the Canadian pianist seemed shy as he bowed to the audience. If he were, no one could have guessed from his playing, which was brilliant from the first note to the last. At the end of the first half, the audience demanded an encore before the intermission, something that is almost unheard of in the concert world. The recital was a huge success. Great things were about to happen.

An Extraordinary Offer

Glenn had made records before this. He and Guerrero had recorded a composition by Mozart when Glenn was about eight years old. In 1953, Glenn had made his first commercial recording, a ten-inch LP on the Hallmark label.

David Oppenheim of Columbia Records had been on the lookout for new talent. He found it in Glenn. The day after the performance, Oppenheim contacted Walter Homburger to offer Glenn a three-year recording contract. The contract would allow Glenn to choose his own music. This was unheard of. Columbia had never before contracted a musician after a debut recital.

Every young musician dreams of just such an offer, but if they were to get one, most would choose to play it safe by recording something familiar to most listeners, perhaps some Mozart or Chopin. Not Glenn. He selected music unfamiliar to much of the record-buying public: the *Goldberg Variations* by Johann Sebastian Bach.

THE
TOWN
HALL

THE·TOWN·HALL
THE·LEAGUE·FOR·POLITICAL
1894   EDUCATION
YE·SHALL·KNOW·THE·TRUTH·AND
THE·TRUTH·SHALL·MAKE·YOU·FREE

THE
TOWN
HALL

The Town Hall, Inc., internationally renowned recital hall; sponsor, since 1894, of a celebrated Morning Lecture Series; producer of the nation's favorite radio forum, "America's Town Meeting of the Air"; scene of study courses and seminars offered through its Short Course Division.

ALFRED SCOTT, *Publisher*, 156 Fifth Avenue, New York.   129-1-11E-55

Glenn's Hero

Bach was known for his mastery of counterpoint, a compositional technique that combines two or more melodies at the same time. For example, the song "Row Your Boat" can be sung as a round by two, three or more voices. However, a "round" is a very simple example of counterpoint. Bach's use of counterpoint was far more complex, with many different melodies interwoven at the same time. Many of his fugues, a type of composition, are brilliant examples of counterpoint.

In counterpoint, each melody is as important as all the others. The difficulty for a pianist playing Bach is to bring out these melodies so the listener can hear them clearly. Glenn was a master at doing just that. His mathematical mind loved the puzzles presented by this compositional technique.

Glenn admired J.S. Bach, whom he called the world's most extraordinary musician. Glenn believed that Bach was a non-conformist who wrote music the way he wanted to. Bach was true to his own vision and made no effort to be fashionable. Glenn, of course, was also a non-conformist.

The master's music was very important to Glenn's development as a musician. Glenn had known Bach's music since he'd been a little boy and had learned all the pieces in Book One of *The Well-Tempered Clavier*. Therefore, it wasn't too surprising that he decided to play Bach on his first recording. Leave it to Glenn, though, to astonish everyone by choosing to play the *Goldberg Variations*, a set of thirty variations on a theme which together really test a pianist's skill and musicianship.

J. S. Bach (1685-1750) was a German organist and composer of the Baroque era.

Many stories have been told about the *Goldberg Variations*. One tale is that Bach wrote them for a certain Count Hermann Karl von Keyserling in 1741. The count was the Russian ambassador to the Court of Saxony. He had difficulty sleeping, so he asked one of his court musicians, Johann Gottlieb Goldberg, a pupil of Bach's, to ask the famous composer if he would write some soothing music to help him sleep. Bach obliged and used a simple theme he had written years earlier as the basis for a set of thirty very complex variations.

The story goes on to say that the Count was happy with the music. As a reward, he gave Bach a golden goblet with a hundred coins in it.

A person with hypochondria is unusually anxious about their health. Hypochondriacs may fear they have a serious disease, even though doctors tell them they don't. They will often seek diagnosis and treatment even though there is nothing medically wrong with them.

Recording

Glenn recorded the *Goldberg Variations* at Columbia's New York studio. Every day he would arrive with his chair, sweaters, water and assorted pills.

Glenn knew that he would someday be a great success. Confident as he was, though, he probably wasn't prepared for the stress of a major career. As the pressures of performing increased, he began to use medication to help him with stress and with his various physical ailments. He took sedatives to calm his nerves and medication to ease the pain in his back, arms and hands.

He had always worried about his health. Even as a child, he had been afraid of germs, and as he grew older, he became even more fearful for his health. Glenn was very honest and would tell people that he was terrified of catching a cold or getting ill.

His illnesses were chronic. Whether they were real or imagined, no one really knew. He kept detailed records of his pain and visited many doctors. Maybe he was a hypochondriac, someone who imagines being ill. Real or not, his illness caused him problems and forced him to cancel many concerts. In fact, he developed a reputation for cancelling at the last minute.

The World
Takes Notice

The same year the *Goldberg Variations* record was released, Glenn played for the first time with an American orchestra, the Detroit Symphony.

In 1982, twenty-five years after he first recorded the *Goldberg Variations*, Glenn made a new version of this music. It too became a best-selling album. Many people prefer the earlier version because the tempo was faster, and the playing seemed more daring. The later version is slower, and according to others, more reflective, more mature. Both versions are still available on CD today.

He completed the recording in one week. The results were wonderful. Glenn's unique musicianship and his stunning technical mastery of the keyboard came through in every bar.

The record sold more copies than any other classical record in 1956. It remained in print even after Glenn recorded a new version much later. Glenn's interpretation of the *Goldberg Variations* brought him instant fame. This recording, together with the coming concert tour, would change his life dramatically.

"The musical genius is a nut" by Duncan MacPherson,
The Toronto Star, Saturday, April 11, 1981

Glenn's mannerisms at the keyboard could be very distracting. Many critics and audiences found them off-putting. But people grew to love this peculiar man who fidgeted while he played and dressed warmly even in the heat of summer. This caricature by famed Canadian cartoonist Duncan MacPherson is an affectionate portrait of Glenn.

The Perfect Piano

Because Glenn's hearing was so sensitive, he was always on the lookout for the perfect piano. He was rarely satisfied with any instrument he played. Fortunately, he finally found a piano that more or less matched the

one he heard in his mind's ear. It was a Steinway piano and became known by its model number CD318. Glenn found it in 1960 and played it for years. Unfortunately, piano movers dropped it in 1972, and it was never the same again. Glenn purchased a Yamaha grand piano in 1981.

Glenn choosing a piano at the Steinway studios in New York City

A Very Difficult Year: 1956-1957 Concerts

As well as achieving great acclaim for his public performances during this time, Glenn also gained fame as a promising young composer. His String Quartet Opus I was performed by the Montreal String Quartet with Glenn on piano. The music received very positive reviews.

Glenn, just twenty-four, was suddenly becoming famous. People who had never heard of him had bought the Goldberg recording and now wanted to hear him live. Glenn was about to find out what touring was like. His first concert schedule took him throughout the United States, Canada and to Europe.

The life of a concert artist is glamorous. It's also lonely and tiring. Performers have to travel constantly. The food is often bad, hotel rooms can be lonely, and the anxiety level is high. Touring takes its toll on even the hardiest musicians. Many have damaged their hands from overuse or succumbed to illness as a result of stress.

Glenn was not a strong man physically. He also didn't like crowds, and he was not keen on travelling. He rarely spent any time sightseeing.

Although he had enjoyed performing when he was a teenager, the risks now were much greater and the audiences far more critical. The pressure to play brilliantly every time was intense. He later said this was one of the most difficult years of his entire life.

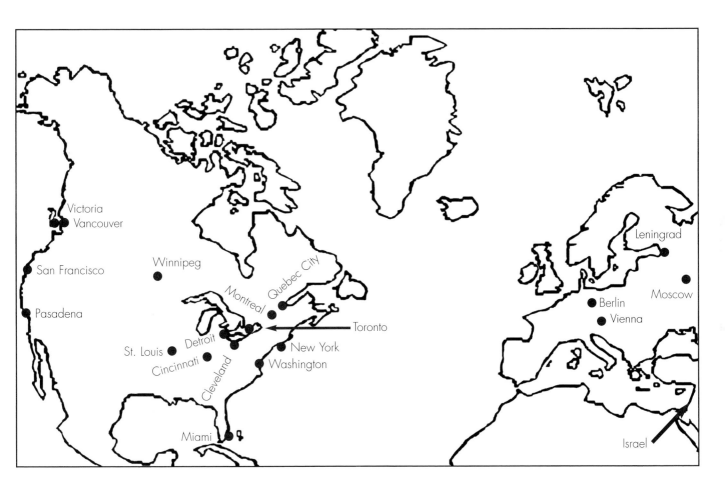

During the 1956-57 concert seasons, Glenn played in Detroit, New York, Windsor, Hamilton, Toronto, Stratford, Winnipeg, St. Louis, Montreal, Vancouver, Niagara Falls, Quebec, San Francisco, Pasadena, Victoria, Cleveland, Moscow, Leningrad (now St. Petersburg), Berlin, Vienna, Hollywood, Washington, Syracuse, Cincinnati and Miami. The following year, 1958, was just as hectic. During this year he also traveled to Jerusalem, Tel Aviv and Haifa, three cities in Israel.

East meets West

The Soviet Union and North America were engaged in what was called the Cold War. In the Soviet Union at that time, certain kinds of music, art and literature of the 20th century were forbidden because the government believed they were decadent and would have a corrupting influence on the people.

While he was on his first major concert tour, Glenn was invited to play in the Soviet Union, in both Moscow and in Leningrad (as St. Petersburg was then called). This was a great honour for Glenn and Canada. He would be the first Canadian musician, and the first North American pianist, to play in that country. Glenn accepted. But even in Russia, he created a bit of controversy.

His concerts in Moscow and Leningrad were a huge success. Glenn captured the hearts of the Russian people, who showered him with bouquets of flowers and applause. Crowds appeared everywhere he went. Extra chairs were placed on the stage so more people could hear him play.

He also agreed to play for the students at the Moscow Conservatory on the condition that he be allowed to play anything he wanted. He chose music by Arnold Schoenberg, Anton Webern and

The Winter Palace in Leningrad (now St. Petersburg)

Glenn had been influenced by Schoenberg's music as a teenager. The Austrian-born composer was a man whose vision of music differed greatly from the visions of those who had come before him. He developed a new style of composing called the twelve-tone system, which Glenn used in some of his own music.

Ernst Krenek, composers whose music was frowned upon in that country.

Glenn wanted these students to hear music that had not been played in Russia for many years. In his struggle for perfection, he was always looking for music that was not often performed, or that others did not particularly like. He wanted people to challenge themselves the way he challenged himself.

Many of the students at the concert were annoyed. A few people walked out. Although Glenn made some of them uncomfortable, he certainly enjoyed himself. He was like a great teacher who can't wait to share his discoveries. Soon, the world would become his classroom.

A poster announcing Glenn's concert in Moscow

Another Trial

Herbert von Karajan was one of the most famous and respected conductors of the 20th century. To many people he was a heroic figure. Some people called him the "General Music Director of Europe." He towered over the music scene as conductor of the Berlin Philharmonic, which many believed he had made into the best orchestra in the world.

After he had astounded the Russians, Glenn travelled to Germany, where he performed with the Berlin Philharmonic Orchestra, led by Herbert von Karajan. Glenn faced a great test again. German audiences know the music of Beethoven and Bach very well. After all, both were German composers. Glenn's playing was magical and touched the hearts of his audiences. He also earned the respect of the great conductor, who believed that Glenn was ahead of his time.

Glenn arriving in Berlin

Command Central

Now in his late twenties, Glenn decided it was time to move. He'd tried living for a short time on an estate outside Toronto and found it too domesticated for him. He'd also stayed for a while at a hotel in the city. This, too, wasn't satisfactory. He needed a place where he could live as he wanted without having to worry much about looking after it. When he returned from his first overseas international tour, he moved into a six-room penthouse apartment.

The balcony of Glenn's apartment building on St. Clair Avenue in Toronto

Music manuscripts, books, records and tapes were strewn all over the place. Empty orange juice and milk cartons and boxes of arrowroot cookies were everywhere. He also kept his beloved old Chickering piano there. When he had visitors, he'd warn them not to lean against it, because it might break.

It was a messy apartment, but it was home base. He lived the life of a creative artist who followed his own dreams. He spent much time alone, because he needed the time to think, write and play. His world was one of music and ideas. Glenn was very private and demanded that people respect his privacy. He once fired a cleaning lady because she gossiped about him.

Over time, he developed the reputation of being a recluse, even though he wasn't. He was in touch with the world by phone, through radio and TV, and through his writing. He made many friends. People liked Glenn. They accepted his eccentric lifestyle because he was brilliant, funny, kind and interesting.

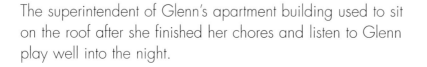

The superintendent of Glenn's apartment building used to sit on the roof after she finished her chores and listen to Glenn play well into the night.

Glenn didn't consider himself to be only a pianist. He was a creative artist, someone with vision and the courage to dream. Glenn believed that the composer and pianist were really co-creators of a piece of music. He didn't like the idea that the musician was someone who only reproduced what the composer had written. Instead, he argued that the musician should try to find something in the music that no one had heard before. This was a difficult point for many people to understand and accept.

Another Risk

Glenn's contract with CBS called for three records in two years. It was time for record number two. The first had been a surprising success. Could he do it again so soon?

Glenn chose to record Beethoven's last three sonatas, very serious pieces usually played by more mature and experienced pianists. A few people raised their eyebrows, but Glenn had made up his mind. This was the music he would record, and that was that.

He played the sonatas at a quicker tempo than listeners were used to. This time the critics were not pleased. The comments were cutting. One thought Glenn's playing childish; another thought it lacked any substance; a third said that Glenn would look back on this record with regret.

Glenn, who hated criticism, was hurt and refused to admit he may have misjudged. He argued that a creative artist must try to find different ways of interpreting familiar music.

Glenn made up for this record when he recorded his successful version of Beethoven's Piano Concerto No. 2 with Leonard Bernstein and the New York Philharmonic.

Growing Turmoil
1958

Glenn often forgot to return the keys to hotel rooms where he stayed, and, over the years, accidentally developed a collection.

Although Glenn was now a highly respected pianist, he was also growing more and more unhappy with performing. He had enjoyed it as a teenager, but this was far more stressful.

Like his parents, though, Glenn had a strong sense of duty, and this made him keep on. Still, the inner conflict must have been almost unbearable at times. Perhaps by now his ideas about playing in public were fully formed. Even this early in his concert career, Glenn probably preferred to stay home. However, someone with his talent is very much in demand. He once said, "Who said this was supposed to be fun anyway?"

Sometimes when people are under a lot of pressure, they become ill. In Stockholm, Sweden, he grew quite ill with something like the flu and collapsed. After convalescing in a hotel in Hamburg, Germany, he managed to carry on with the tour, which proved to be a huge success.

Of course, every musician occasionally has a bad day. On this tour, Glenn was booed by an audience in Florence, Italy, because he played music by Schoenberg. Actually, according to Glenn, it was only the people in the upper balcony who booed. The lower levels

The concert in Jerusalem took place in December. Glenn found it quite cold. The Israelis placed heaters on the stage to keep Glenn warm while he played.

applauded madly, and he milked it for all it was worth, receiving five or six curtain calls.

After this, he flew to Israel, where he performed in Tel Aviv and Jerusalem. Israel in 1958 was a very young country, and Glenn was a young man not yet at the height of his career. The Israelis, like the Germans and the Russians, embraced him instantly. They adored his playing.

A Pat on the Back

Steinway & Sons is one of the world's most famous piano manufacturers. Glenn used to spend a lot of time there trying out pianos.

One incident during these years shows just how frustrated Glenn was becoming with performing and also reveals his extreme sensitivity to physical contact. Glenn was at Steinway & Sons, the famous piano company headquartered in New York.

Glenn was testing a piano when the head technician walked by and touched Glenn, who exclaimed that the man hurt him. Later he sued Steinway, claiming the technician had shaken his hand too strongly and that he had hurt his back by placing his forearms on it. Glenn claimed he could no longer perform concerts. At one point, he complained so much about the pain that his doctor encased his arm and shoulder in a plaster cast.

One witness later said that the technician had simply patted Glenn lightly on the back. The media played up the story. Steinway settled with Glenn out of court.

No one knows for sure just what happened. Perhaps the man simply patted Glenn on the back as a gesture of welcome. Glenn, already tired and sick of playing concerts, was probably even more sensitive than usual and reacted to the man's touch.

Certainly, the doctors couldn't find anything really wrong. Maybe this was a case of Glenn's hypochondria playing tricks on him again. Glenn did resume playing concerts, but the feeling of discontent only worsened.

The Turning Point

This drawing of Glenn Gould was drawn by the very famous American artist Al Hirschfeld.

From the American debuts on, Glenn's fame spread. Yet he often said he would retire by the time he was thirty-five. No one believed him. Sometimes, people weren't sure if Glenn were teasing or not. After all, who would dare give up a well-paying performing career and the respect and affection of audiences all over the world?

The fact is he loved to play, but grew to dislike live concerts. He especially resented playing concertos with an orchestra because he felt it was a battle between the pianist and the other musicians, like gladiators in an arena. Live performances were heartless and senseless. He felt cheapened when he played in public. He believed the artist was trying to communicate to listeners who sat there like spectators in an arena, hoping something would go wrong.

Glenn rarely attended other people's concerts. When he did, he would listen from the wings because sitting in the audience made him feel claustrophobic. He didn't attend plays for the same reason, but he liked movies and found the movie theater a comforting place, probably because it was dark, and he could choose an isolated seat.

He was also convinced that the concert hall was becoming obsolete because recording technology was becoming so sophisticated. He argued that people would someday simply stop attending concerts, preferring to listen to music in the comfort of their own home.

Glenn was a perfectionist who wanted to play music the way he heard it in his mind. Concerts didn't allow a musician to make corrections or to replay a passage in different ways. The performer has one chance and that's it.

As well, he wanted to do other things. He considered himself to be more than just a pianist. He was a creative artist, a visionary, who needed time and solitude to think, compose, write and experiment.

Absolute Opposites

Many people never understood Glenn's dislike of performing in public. They were used to pianists like Arthur Rubinstein who loved the stage. A charming man with a halo of white hair, the Polish pianist looked like an aristocrat sitting at the piano, graceful fingers caressing the keys, eyes closed, head thrown back in ecstasy.

Rubinstein believed his playing communicated with the very soul of his audience. Glenn had no use for that idea. Once, he and Rubinstein discussed performing. Rubinstein was as puzzled as everyone else by Glenn's dislike of the concert stage. Glenn probably didn't understand why Rubinstein loved to perform so much. Rubinstein said Glenn would return to the stage. Glenn said he would not.

At the end of their conversation, Rubinstein was not convinced and refused to believe that Glenn would never perform again. He was wrong. Yet, though these two brilliant musicians were absolute opposites in their attitudes to performing and to audiences, each contributed greatly to people's love of music.

Rubinstein said about himself and Glenn, "We are absolute opposites."

71

Telephone Message

4-F 62
19

TIME 150 P M

M ~ ackeghew

ROOM 1007

The following message was received during your absence from

M

Tel. No. Leonard Bernstein
called.

Edna

WELL INFORMED TRAVELERS COME FROM ALL OVER THE WORLD

THE STANHOPE

995 Fifth Avenue
New York 28, N. Y.

A few of the headlines from newspapers of the time read as follows:

WHO'S THE BOSS—CONDUCTOR OR SOLOIST? (New York Herald Tribune)

BRAHMS IS BEATEN (New York Journal)

GOULD GETS HIS KNUCKLES RAPPED (Toronto Telegram)

GOULD, BERNSTEIN AT ODDS ON BRAHMS (Words and Music)

Who's the Boss 1962

Glenn's willingness to take a chance with interpretation was by now legendary. In one of the most famous incidents of his concert career, he disagreed completely with his friend, Leonard Bernstein, who for many years was the conductor of the great New York Philharmonic Orchestra and one of the most respected musicians in the world.

Glenn was to play the Brahms Piano Concerto No.1 in D Minor, Opus 15, a very well-known piece. During rehearsal, Glenn informed Leonard Bernstein that he wanted to play it at a slower tempo than normal. Although Bernstein disagreed, he graciously accepted Glenn's decision. He probably knew Glenn well enough to know that it would be impossible to change the young man's mind.

Just before the performance, however, Bernstein made a now famous speech in which he told the audience that while he respected Glenn's artistry and courage, he did not agree with the pianist's interpretation. Glenn, ever-gracious, was not in the least offended by Bernstein's remarks.

Glenn's father made this chair. It was a simple folding chair. Mr. Gould attached special brass fittings to its legs and added screws so Glenn could adjust the height. Glenn took the chair everywhere. After several years, it got really worn and rickety. Often it would creak when he leaned back in it.

George Szell was a brilliant conductor who could be bad-tempered at times. He was also someone who recognized genius in others. After one of Glenn's concerts he said, "That nut's a genius."

A Funny Story, True or Not

Wherever he played, whether on stage or in the studio, Glenn was extremely fussy about the height of his chair in relation to the piano keyboard. Usually, he could get the right height simply by adjusting the folding chair his father had altered for him. Once, though, he couldn't.

At a rehearsal with the Cleveland Symphony Orchestra and its conductor George Szell, Glenn just couldn't get comfortable at the keyboard. He asked a carpenter to make some blocks and place them under the piano legs. All of this happened during the rehearsal break, of course. But it took some time.

Szell grew very frustrated with Glenn. Later, a local paper reported that the conductor had said to Glenn, "Perhaps if I were to slice one-sixteenth of an inch off your derrière, Mr. Gould, we could begin." Glenn denied that Szell had spoken so rudely to him and added that he would have left the stage immediately if the conductor had said any such thing.

The Last Concert

The Wilshire Ebell Theatre

Glenn quit playing concerts the same year the Beatles came to New York and played in Carnegie Hall and the following year at Shea Stadium, home of the New York Mets. The pop music scene was never the same again. Millions of young people in North America fell in love with the British rockers. Popular music began to dominate the airwaves during the 1960s. Groups like The Rolling Stones, The Who and The Grateful Dead became extremely popular, as did singer/songwriters like Bob Dylan and Canadians Joni Mitchell and Neil Young.

During his years of touring, Glenn talked frequently about quitting. He often felt ill. He was not happy. Despite all the warning signs, no one, not even his agent Walter Homburger, suspected that on the night of April 10, 1964, Glenn would give his last live public performance on a concert stage.

Maybe Glenn himself didn't really know until that night. Maybe he didn't even know that night. But it was his last time on a concert stage. When the final note sounded in the Wilshire Ebell Theatre in Los Angeles, he looked at the audience, smiled mysteriously, bowed and left the stage.

He made no grand announcement to the papers. He simply withdrew. It took some time before people realized that Glenn had stopped performing. Many expected he would come back at some point and resume his concert career. Even Homburger kept making plans. Glenn, however, didn't return. He was thirty-two years old and had other things to do.

The Future

Swing dancing was very popular with young people from the mid 1930s until the mid 1950s, when rock and roll began to dominate the popular music scene. People who were really into dancing to swing bands were called "jitterbugs". Tommy Dorsey, Benny Goodman and Count Basie were famous swing musicians.

Glenn believed that in the future musicians would write, record and edit their own music. In other words, they would completely control their creative work. In fact, that's what groups like the Beatles began to do after their initial hit records. The Beatles' *Sgt. Pepper's Lonely Hearts Club Band* is a good example of musicians being involved in every stage of the writing and recording process. Although the Beatles had millions of fans all over the world, Glenn didn't care much for their music. He preferred popular singers like Barbra Streisand and Petula Clark, and he also enjoyed swing music in small doses.

The 1960s were a time of great social and political upheaval. Young people demonstrated at universities and on the streets protesting the Vietnam War and unequal treatment of women and minorities. In the United States, thousands of people took part in marches protesting against racism.

Although Glenn was very busy with his music, he was aware of these movements and most likely agreed with people who were protesting against violence and discrimination. Glenn, of course, had no use for war. He also wanted people to be free to express themselves in whatever way suited them. He was especially concerned about children and how they were treated. He used to say that adults should love children and encourage them to be whatever they wanted to be.

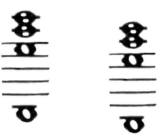

What Now–Again?

Glenn receiving a doctorate in 1964, the year he left the concert stage.

At only thirty-two years of age, Glenn had given up a well-paid career. He was earning approximately $3,000 per concert, a substantial sum of money back in the early 1960s. He could easily gross about $100,000 annually. It's not easy giving up that kind of money.

What would replace that income? Of course, Glenn was really not that interested in money. It was more important to him to do things on his own terms. But what to do?

If he wasn't completely sure how the next stage of his life would unfold, he knew one thing for certain—no more travel. He'd had enough of the pressure, of criticism of his keyboard mannerisms and of the endless round of hotels, trains and planes.

As it turned out, Glenn really did have a master plan. He'd had it since he was about twenty, and he'd been telling people about it for years. It wasn't his fault that many of them hadn't been listening. He had planned to stop playing concerts at thirty and to record until he was fifty.

Glenn believed in change because there were so many things to do, and he had the talent, the drive and the intelligence to do them. So why not? He was sticking to his master plan. It was time for a change.

And what a change it was.

What Does Glenn Really Want to Do?

Glenn retreated to the cottage, where he recharged his batteries. With the exception of a few speaking engagements, he kept mostly to himself, reading, walking and thinking a great deal. This period was very important to him, as critical as the time years earlier when he'd quit his music lessons and taken refuge at the cottage to ready himself for the future. Now, he was again preparing himself for an uncertain future.

While he was at the cottage, he probably often asked himself this question: What do I really want to do? Of course, he'd been asking that question all his life. Others had wondered, too. Some might even have felt that Glenn should be happy being a brilliant pianist. That would be more than enough for most. Not Glenn. He was so good at so many things.

So what was he? Was he a brilliant pianist? composer? radio and TV personality? writer? philosopher? The answer is that he was all of these and more. Glenn had always known in his heart that he wanted to do much more than just play the piano in public. Early on he had shown talent for writing and composing. Recording technology fascinated him.

Glenn could work on one thing and think about and plan several other things at the same time. He could study a score,

Glenn wanted to be in charge of everything he did, whether it was playing the piano, composing, conducting, even interviews. If a writer asked for an interview, Glenn wanted the person to send him a list of questions in advance.

Glenn had great respect for people who went their own way. Two men whom he admired greatly were Marshall McLuhan and Leopold Stokowski. Both men were ahead of their time. McLuhan, a Canadian, wrote about how technology and communication change the way we perceive the world. Stokowski was a famous conductor who, like Glenn, believed in the growing importance of recording technology. Stokowski was the man who conducted the music to Walt Disney's famous movie, *Fantasia*.

Marshall McLuhan

memorizing it without sitting at the piano and at the same time talk about something else.

Still, what would he do next? Teaching was out. Glenn never taught in the formal sense like many other musicians. He said he was afraid of teaching because it was a huge responsibility. Yet, in his own way, he had always taught, from the time he was small and had lectured his friends about music.

Even though he spent much of his time alone, Glenn also needed to share his enthusiasm for ideas with everyone. He was a great communicator, a bit of a ham at times, whether at the piano keyboard, in front of an orchestra, behind a radio mike, in front of a TV camera, or in a chair talking with a friend or associate. Ideas poured out of him.

Now that he had retired from the stage, he was ready to pursue all of his interests wholeheartedly. And he was ready to share his thoughts with everyone. He would become an inspiring teacher, not of piano students, but of the public. He could now commit himself fully to exploring all the ideas that mattered to him. He could be a creative artist completely on his own terms. The years 1964 to 1982 would be in many ways the most productive of his life. As always, though, he would spend them on his own terms. He had to be in complete control of his life.

A True Romance

Performing on stage, a musician plays a piece, mistakes and all. The musician can't stop to make corrections. Recording lets a musician edit and splice. Glenn called this "creative cheating", and he was completely in favour of it. Many people disagreed with this process and thought it was plain cheating.

Glenn thought he could earn his living at least in part by recording. He had been making records since his American debut. Now he began to record even more.

He continued travelling to New York to record until 1971. After that he recorded in a studio at Eaton Auditorium in Toronto, the same place where he had made his debut on organ years earlier.

Not surprisingly, Glenn devoted himself completely to recording. The music of Bach would remain important to his music making, but over the years he recorded works by Mozart, Beethoven, Schoenberg and many others.

He made more than eighty records for CBS Masterworks/Sony Classical during these years. He must have surprised even himself. It takes a lot of preparation to make even one good record. Glenn, ever the perfectionist, was perhaps more demanding than most musicians. Yet he produced an enormous body of recorded work.

Glenn working in the studio

In the Studio

Glenn's desire to make lots of records should not have surprised anyone. His fascination with recording technology had begun early in life. As a youngster, he'd experimented with sound. He and a friend would run a string between two cans and send messages. He also attached microphones to his old Chickering piano. When he was in his teens, he spent time at the CBC, where what he called his "love affair" with sound began. Glenn was also one of the first people in Toronto to own a tape recorder. He became as knowledgeable about the technical aspects of recording as many of the engineers and technicians who worked with him.

In the recording studio, he could perfect his music in isolation. There was no audience, except for a few technicians. In his struggle for perfection, he could record a piece as many times as he liked, then edit it until he was satisfied.

Glenn developed his own philosophy about recording. He imagined a day when musicians no longer performed on the stage. Instead, they would make many records, and people would stay home to listen to them in comfort. Some would even make their own records by taking the best bits from a variety of recordings of the same piece by several different performers.

The Great Test: Glenn believed most people couldn't tell if a record had been edited or not. To prove this, he devised a test. He made a tape and asked several people to identify where the tape had been spliced. The musicians scored the lowest.

Today almost all classical performers record. CDs and DVDs are sold by the millions annually. Many people are very familiar with recording technology, and make their own CDs right on their home computer. Music is now part of the electronic highway. Glenn would probably nod his head and smile.

Glenn the Composer

Timothy Findley, the renowned Canadian writer, once referred to Glenn as one of the "god-people" because the pianist was so brilliant and so talented as to be god-like.

Glenn was famous for his use of the telephone. He spent hours on it, running up incredibly high long-distance charges. He was always the one who called, and the call could come at any time of day, and especially night. He could talk for hours, then suddenly hang up.

Glenn had composed ever since he was a child. Of course, most of those pieces were written for his music classes at the Conservatory. As a young man of eighteen, he had composed his Sonata for Bassoon and Piano. Several years later, in his early twenties, he composed a String Quartet. He also composed "So You Want to Write a Fugue" and some other pieces that were never published.

Yet after his retirement from the concert stage, Glenn really did not compose much music, even though he had the time. He started many compositions and never finished them, saying once that he specialized in unfinished pieces. This must have frustrated him enormously on occasion.

Maybe he simply knew too much about music and couldn't settle on a particular style of composing. Or maybe he compared himself to other composers and felt he didn't measure up. He was after all a perfectionist in everything he did.

Glenn did arrange music for the film *Slaughterhouse-Five*, based on the novel by Kurt Vonnegut, and for the film *The Wars*, based on a novel by Timothy Findley. As well, music by Bach played by Glenn was used for the animated film, *Spheres*, and for the movie, *The Terminal Man*.

The Scribe

Glenn wrote many essays on a variety of topics and people. These were collected and made into a book, *The Glenn Gould Reader.*

Glenn had always written the liner notes for his own records. In fact, he won a Grammy award for the notes to one of his albums. He said many times that he would like to write a novel someday. After his retirement, he continued to write essays and liner notes for his records. He also wrote scripts for his radio and TV productions. He never did write a novel.

The Canadian Broadcasting Corporation was launched in 1936. Glenn was four years old and soon became an avid fan. At eighteen, he made his first live broadcast on CBC Radio. He went on to make more than one hundred and fifty broadcasts and appearances on CBC Radio and Television. The Corporation was like a second home to him. He even had an office there.

One writer compared listening to one of these documentaries with sitting on a train during rush hour, reading a paper, overhearing several people talking while a radio blares somewhere in the train car accompanied by the sound of the train's wheels.

Glenn was able to keep track of many different things at the same time. And of course, he loved playing fugues, which make use of counterpoint. He was always experimenting, always thinking of different ways of doing things. So now it seems only natural that he imagined using techniques used by composers and adapting them to radio documentaries.

The Radio and TV Star

During the 1960s and 1970s, the CBC offered Glenn plenty of opportunity to put his many talents to wonderful use. He wrote, produced and acted in many documentaries on different topics such as contemporary music, the television documentary *Toronto,* produced by John McGreevy, and radio documentaries on Newfoundland and the Mennonites.

Glenn loved Canada. A friend of his wrote that whenever the topic of Canada came up in conversation, Glenn became boyishly enthusiastic. He was in awe of this country's natural beauty, its vastness and its people. He believed Canadians to be very cultivated people. He also had great respect for people who lived in those remote regions that stretched all the way to the Arctic Circle.

In the late sixties, he developed a radio documentary that brought him much acclaim—*The Idea of North*, which was the first of three documentaries that came to be called *Glenn Gould's Solitude Trilogy.*

All his life solitude was important to Glenn. Perhaps that is why he was fascinated with the North, a place with vast expanses and few people, a place that is quiet and where life

Some of Glenn's well-known radio and TV work includes the following broadcasts and TV shows:

The Art of Glenn Gould
The Well-Tempered Listener
Stokowski: A Portrait for Radio
Glenn Gould's Toronto

can be hard. As a boy, he had pored over maps of the north and later studied aerial photographs. Glenn wanted to understand how people in these regions lived, how they got along, how they survived, what kinds of lives they made for themselves.

Ever the innovator, Glenn invented a novel approach to recording this documentary. He called it the "contrapuntal documentary". His technique involved interweaving background sounds and human voices. Some people were skeptical that this approach would work, but Glenn knew it would and he proved it.

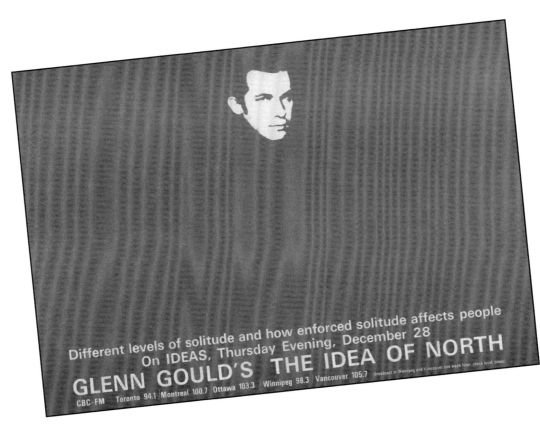

Different levels of solitude and how enforced solitude affects people
On IDEAS, Thursday Evening, December 28
GLENN GOULD'S THE IDEA OF NORTH
CBC-FM   Toronto 94.1 / Montreal 100.7 / Ottawa 103.3 / Winnipeg 98.3 / Vancouver 105.7 (broadcast in Winnipeg and Vancouver one week later, check local times)

The Several Mr. Goulds

Glenn as Theodore Slutz

Glenn greatly enjoyed writing and lecturing about music, but he didn't simply stand behind a lectern and pontificate. He invented several personalities or alter egos, and through them he spoke and wrote about music.

As Herbert von Hochmeister, German critic, Glenn had published articles about music even before he quit the stage. Other personalities he invented were: Sir Nigel Twitt-Thornwaite, Dean of the British conductors; S. E. Lemming, MD, and Wolfgang von Krankmeister, psychiatrists. He also invented Theodore Slutz of Brooklyn Heights and his alter ego, Myron Chianti, a character based on the famous movie actor Marlon Brando, known for his portrayal of Don Corleone in the film *The Godfather*.

Glenn used these personalities to great effect. He had a terrific sense of humour, although he once admitted that he needed to assume different identities to be funny. Of course, even when Glenn was being funny, he was completely serious about what he was doing. Everything he did during these years he did because he was searching, striving to understand the world around him.

Glenn's Mother Dies

When Florence Gould died, Glenn wrote her obituary. In it, he described how his mother had been attracted to church music even as a teenager. As an adult, she devoted her talents primarily to music for the sacred service. Over the years, she served as a soloist in large Toronto choirs. She also was the organist in a central Presbyterian church and choir leader at the Uxbridge United Church. Mrs. Gould taught piano and vocal music in Toronto, Uxbridge and Bradford, Ontario. Glenn ended his obituary with the following words: "Florence Gould was a woman of tremendous faith, and wherever she went, she strove to instill that faith in others."

Life during these years was good for Glenn. He was involved in many projects. He reached thousands of people regularly through radio, recordings, TV and writing. Always in the background was his mother. She was his rock. Glenn often spoke with her and confided in her.

In July of 1975, a very sad event took place. Mr. Gould came home from work. When his wife opened the door for him, he saw her start to collapse. He caught her before she hit the floor. Mrs. Gould had suffered a stroke.

She was taken to the hospital where she lay unconscious for five days before she died. Glenn called her doctor every day, asking for advice about specialists and treatment. He was extremely upset and worried.

His mother was eighty-three years of age when she died and had lived long enough to see her prediction, that Glenn would be a famous pianist, come true. She had been extremely proud of him.

As Glenn was a very private person, he didn't say much to anyone about her death, which had nevertheless affected him very deeply. She had been his teacher, his mentor and probably his greatest fan. He had remained close to her through all his successes and trials, and never really got over her death.

A Loyal Son

A few years later, Mr. Gould decided to remarry and asked his son to be his best man. Glenn wanted his father to be happy and content. At the same time, he also remained very loyal to his mother's memory. He was torn. He struggled for some time with his father's request. It must have been difficult to reach a decision. Even so, he decided that he couldn't honour Bert's invitation.

Glenn mailed his father a letter, which he'd rewritten several times, wishing Bert and his bride-to-be, Vera Dobson, all the best, but said he could not attend the wedding. No doubt, this was a very difficult thing to do. Glenn, however, never shied away from what he believed was right.

The End

After Florence's death in 1975, Glenn carried on with his busy schedule. There were so many more things to do, ideas to explore, records to make. Glenn had been thinking about conducting too and had even put together a small group of musicians.

His health, however, was not good. He had trouble with his back. He also experienced chest pain and heat in his arms. Friends noticed that he was looking older and sicklier. Sometimes he had difficulty playing the piano. Glenn had also been taking all kinds of medication and sedatives for many years. These could not have helped his general health.

He'd never been a particularly strong man physically. Since childhood he'd worried about germs, drafts and colds. As a young performer on tour throughout the 1950s and early 1960s, he'd suffered much pain, especially in his hands and back. Perhaps that early injury at the cottage so many years before had contributed in some way to his problems. No one knows for certain.

Even during the last year when Glenn's health was at its worst, he was making plans for more projects. He'd told Jessie he wanted to write an historical novel set in Scotland. He had plans to record all the Beethoven concerti. He dreamed of starting an animal shelter in the Arctic. He also told one friend that he was going to stop playing the piano and devote himself to writing and conducting.

On September 25, 1982, Glenn was supposed to attend a birthday party in his honour. He didn't feel well, so he stayed home, spending the day on the phone with friends. Two days later, his left arm was numb, and he slurred words when he spoke. His friend, Ray Roberts, drove him to Toronto General Hospital, where the doctors diagnosed a stroke.

He asked Ray to call his cousin Jessie, who came immediately. Glenn felt that he would not leave the hospital, even though his cousin tried to tell him he would get well again. Unfortunately, Glenn was right. Two days later he had a second stroke and never regained consciousness. Glenn Gould died on October 4, 1982.

Glenn was buried next to his mother in Mount Pleasant Cemetery, in Toronto, his grave marked with a simple granite plaque. His grave is visited by many people from Canada and around the world.

Glenn loved people and animals. His will testifies to his great compassion for both. Glenn bequeathed his estate to the Salvation Army and to the Toronto Humane Society.

There is a special tree with a plaque dedicated to Glenn in the cemetery, near where he is buried

Canada Mourns

People were shocked when Glenn died. After all, he was a relatively young man at just fifty years old, and he had become a major part of Canada's musical tapestry. Canadians had gotten used to this gentle genius with the quirky sense of humor who could speak about the most complex ideas as easily as he could poke fun at himself.

Glenn once said he thought no one would attend his funeral when he died. How wrong he was. He was much loved. More than three thousand people paid their last respects at Glenn's memorial service at St. Paul's Anglican Church in Toronto. Flowers and tributes came from people like opera star Elisabeth Schwarzkopf, pianist Vladimir Horowitz, violinist Lord Yehudi Menuhin, and conductors Leonard Bernstein and Herbert von Karajan. Many government officials and adoring fans also attended the service.

The World Recognizes Glenn Gould

Shortly after his death, Glenn was inducted into the Canadian Music Hall of Fame and the National Academy of Recording Arts and Sciences Hall of Fame. Filmmakers, too, have recognized his great contribution. The CBC made a wonderful documentary about him: *Glenn Gould: A Portrait.* Actor Colm Feore portrays Glenn in *Thirty-Two Short Films About Glenn Gould.*

Other forms of recognition include a composition in his honour by Canadian composer Alexina Louie and a Glenn Gould conference. The Royal Conservatory renamed its Professional School the Glenn Gould Professional School. There is also the Glenn Gould Foundation, which offers the international Glenn Gould Prize, a $50,000 prize awarded every three years.

Previous winners are R. Murray Schafer, Yehudi Menuhin, Oscar Peterson, Toru Takemitsu, Yo-Yo Ma and Pierre Boulez.

While he was alive, many musicians commented on Glenn's amazing talent, especially on his unique ability to interpret the music of Johann Sebastian Bach. Two of the twentieth century's musical giants, Leonard Bernstein and Herbert von Karajan, had said that Glenn was a musical genius. Indeed, von Karajan believed that Glenn was a musician of the future, a unique thinker who was ahead of his time. Glenn also received numerous honours, including the Canada Council's Molson Prize, the Harriet Cohen Bach Medal and the *diplôme d'honneur*, which was awarded by the Canadian Conference of the Arts.

Now, after his death, the world began to pay even greater tribute to this most unusual man. In fact, the legend of Glenn Gould keeps growing. People today find him as fascinating as ever. They sense that he was a man who was never satisfied with anything less than his absolute best as a creative artist. They admire his life-long struggle for perfection.

Glenn's Juno award, left, and his Grammy, right

Glenn's Special Legacy

Although Glenn was a virtuoso pianist, he was much more than just a technical wizard. He played the most complicated music with stunning technical facility, astounding listeners with the clarity and accuracy of his technique. From the very beginning, however, he also displayed a unique musical intelligence. He found patterns and relationships in the most complex music and made the listener aware of them. He took apart each piece and recreated it with his own special insight and feeling. He discovered beauty in every composition he played.

Glenn experimented with speed and dynamics, often provoking his audience and other musicians with his daring. He made bold claims about famous composers and their music; he avoided playing many of the greats like Chopin and Schumann while praising the work of modern composers like Arnold Schoenberg and Paul Hindemith. Many people disagreed with Glenn's interpretations of great works. Some found his opinions controversial and sometimes outrageous, but no one could claim that they didn't hear something new when they listened to Glenn's music.

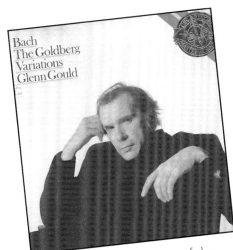

Glenn's 1982 recording of the Goldberg Variations won two GRAMMY awards, a JUNO award and a Gold Disc from the Canadian Recording Industry.

In 1998, Phillips Records compiled a series of recordings by the one hundred finest pianists of the 20th Century. The gentle genius' records form a significant part of this tribute.

To celebrate the 70th anniversary of Glenn Gould's birth, Sony Classical reissued in 2002 a new remastered recording of both versions of the Goldberg Variations. It became the highest selling classical recording in the world.

Bookends

Years earlier as a very young musician, Glenn had achieved world fame with his recording of the *Goldberg Variations*. Shortly before his death at fifty and as a mature musician, he went into the studio to re-record this marvellous music. The world's greatest interpreter of Bach's keyboard works again stunned the world.

This time the music reflected what many believed was a more thoughtful man. The opening aria is much slower, more meditative than the version created by the young man so many years ago. This record, too, achieved instant success. It was also one of the last recordings that Glenn made.

The two records together serve as bookends to Glenn's entire career. The early record made by a young man on the verge of huge success; the later record by a man who was still struggling for perfection.

Glenn Gould

A Chronology of Selected Events

1932	Glenn is born in Toronto at his parents' home on September 25.
1935	The Goulds learn that Glenn is gifted with perfect pitch. Glenn receives his first piano lessons from his mother, Florence Gould. She teaches him until he is ten years old.
1938	On June 5, Glenn gives his first public performance on piano at the Uxbridge United Church. He attends Williamson Road Public School.
1940	Glenn passes his first examination at the Toronto Conservatory of Music (TCM). He earns first class honours in Grade 3 piano. He also begins to study music theory with Leo Smith at TCM.
1942	Glenn begins organ lessons with Frederic K. Silvester at TCM. During the summer he falls at the cottage and injures his back.
1943	Glenn begins piano lessons with Chilean-born pianist and teacher Alberto Guerrero.
1944	In February, Glenn competes in the first Annual Kiwanis Music Festival and wins first prize in the piano trophy competition.
1945	On March 10, Glenn plays on radio for the first time on the program *Kiwanis Festival Winners,* aired by station CFRB. He is awarded the Gordon V. Thompson scholarship at the Kiwanis Music Festival. In June, he passes his piano examination for the TCM Associateship. In September, he enrolls in Malvern Collegiate Institute, and, in December, he gives his first public recital on organ at Eaton Auditorium in Toronto.
1946	Glenn debuts with the Toronto Conservatory Symphony Orchestra at Massey Hall on May 8. In October he receives the TCM Associate Diploma.

1947	Glenn debuts with the Toronto Symphony on January 14, playing Beethoven's Piano Concerto No. 4. The concert takes place in Massey Hall. Later that year, on October 20th, he gives his first solo piano recital in Eaton Auditorium, the same place he performed on organ.
1948	Glenn composes his piano sonata. This is his first major composition.
1950	Glenn performs at the University Of Western Ontario on November 26. This is his first major performance outside his hometown of Toronto. He also composes his second major work, Sonata for Bassoon and Piano. The day before Christmas, he plays piano on CBC Radio. This is his radio debut for the Canadian Broadcasting Corporation, and marks the beginning of a long and happy relationship with the broadcaster.
1951	Glenn performs with the Vancouver Symphony Orchestra at the Orpheum Theatre in Vancouver. He also plays for the Women's Musical Club in Calgary.
1952	Glenn quits his studies with Alberto Guerrero. He also leaves Malvern Collegiate without graduating. He leaves Toronto and goes to the cottage. On September 8, Glenn performs for the first time on CBC-TV. He is the first pianist in Canada to do so.
1953	Glenn performs at Stratford Festival for the first time and gives his first recital in eastern Canada in the Saint John High School Auditorium, Saint John, New Brunswick. He also makes his first commercial record.
1954	On December 14th, he appears with the Montreal Symphony Orchestra at Plateau Hall, Montreal.
1955	Glenn gives two recitals in the United States, the first at the Phillips Gallery in Washington, D.C.; the second at Town Hall in New York. On January 12, he signs his first major recording contract with Columbia. He also finishes composing his String Quartet, Opus 1.

1956	This was an especially significant year for Glenn. His recording of the *Goldberg Variations* is released by Columbia Records. In January he debuts with the Winnipeg Symphony Orchestra, then with the Detroit Symphony. He tours Canada and the United States in the fall.
1957	On January 26, Glenn debuts with the New York Philharmonic Orchestra under the baton of Leonard Bernstein. In March 28, he performs with the Cleveland Symphony. Two months later, in May, he undertakes his first tour of Europe. On May 7, he performs in the Soviet Union in the Moscow State Conservatory.
1958	Glenn tours Austria, Sweden, West Germany, Italy and Israel from August until December.
1959	Glenn is awarded the Harriet Cohn Bach Medal. On August 31, he performs with the Philharmonia Orchestra at the Lucerne Festival in Lucerne, Switzerland. This will be his last concert in Europe.
1960	Glenn rents his famous Steinway piano CD318 for the first time.
1962	Glenn makes several broadcasts on CBC, including one about composer Arnold Schoenberg.
1964	On April 10, Glenn performs at the Wilshire Ebell Theatre in Los Angeles. This will be his last live public performance. On June 10, the University of Toronto awards him an Honorary Doctor of Laws degree. And on November 11, he addresses the Royal Conservatory of Music graduates.
1967	The CBC broadcasts *The Idea of North*, the first part of the Glenn Gould Trilogy. The same year he receives the Canada Molson Prize, and the CBC broadcasts the second part of his trilogy, *The Latecomers*.

1971	Glenn's radio documentary, *Stokowski: A Portrait for Radio,* is aired on the CBC in February.
1972	Glenn arranges the music for the film *Slaughterhouse-Five,* based on the novel by Kurt Vonnegut.
1973	Glenn finally buys his beloved Steinway concert grand, CD318.
1975	Glenn's mother, Florence Gould, dies.
1976	The Canadian Conference of the Arts awards Glenn the *diplôme d'honneur.*
1977	*The Quiet in the Land* airs on the CBC on March 25. This is the third part of his trilogy.
1982	Glenn's second recording of the *Goldberg Variations* is released. The following year, The *Goldberg Variations* wins two Grammy Awards and a JUNO Award the following year.
1982	In August Glenn records the chamber version of Richard Wagner's "Siegfried Idyll" for CBS. This recording marks the beginning of Glenn's new career as a conductor. This is the chamber version of Wagner's famous composition. It is released posthumously in 1990. On October 4, Glenn Gould dies.
1984	The *Goldberg Variations* wins a Gold Disc award given by the Canadian Recording Industry Association.

About the author

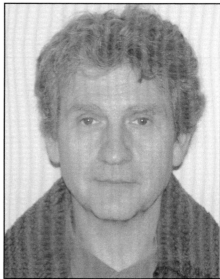

Vladimir Konieczny was born in Germany in 1946, immigrating to Canada with his parents in 1951. As a child, he studied piano and accordion in Toronto, competed in many music festivals and played in clubs during the late 1960s and early 1970s before attending university. A former teacher of English and music for the Vancouver School Board, Vladimir is also an amateur musician who plays flute in a concert band and alto saxophone in a fifteen piece swing band. He first heard Glenn Gould play on CBC Radio in the early 1960s, and became an instant fan, following the pianist's career until his death in 1982.

The author and editors used the following books in researching this story:

Glenn Gould: The Genius and His Music by Lynette Roy (Toronto: Canadian Heroes Series: University of Toronto Press, 1999)

Glenn Gould: A Life and Variations by Otto Friedrich (Toronto: Lester & Orpen Dennys, 1989)

Glenn Gould: Music & Mind by Geoffrey Payzant (Toronto: Van Nostrand Reinhold Ltd., 1978)

Glenn Gould: Variations edited by John McGreevy (Doubleday Canada, 1983)

The Glenn Gould Reader edited by Tim Page (Toronto: Lester & Orpen Dennys, 1984)

The Art of Glenn Gould: Reflections of a Musical Genius by John P. L. Roberts (Toronto: Malcolm Lester Books, 1999)

The Solitary Outlaw: Trudeau, Lewis, Gould, Canetti, McLuhan by B. W. Powe (Toronto: Lester & Orpen Dennys, 1987)

Glenn Gould: The Ecstasy and Tragedy of Genius by Peter F. Ostwald (New York: W.W. Norton & Company, 1997)

Glenn Gould: A Life in Pictures (Toronto: Doubleday Canada, 2002)

Glenn Gould on the Internet

There is quite a lot of information about music and musicians on the internet. More information on Glenn Gould can be found on these sites.

The Official Glenn Gould Website
The official guide to discovering Glenn's life and work
www.glenngould.com

The Glenn Gould Foundation
More resources and information on Glenn, including the International Glenn Gould prize
www.glenngould.ca

The Glenn Gould Archive at the National Archives of Canada
A vast resource containing photographs and papers about and by Glenn
www.nlc-bnc.ca/glenngould

Glenn Gould artist page at Sony Classical, his record label
www.sonyclassical.com/artists/gould

Glenn Gould Studio
Information on the performing and recording venue in Toronto named in Glenn's honour
www.glenngouldstudio.cbc.ca

Glenn Gould: A Perspective
A fan website with resources
http://aix1.uottawa.ca/~weinberg/gould.html

F Minor
Contains writings and works by and about Glenn Gould
www.rci.rutgers.edu/~mwatts/glenn

Note: The internet changes every day. At the time that this book was printed, all of these sites were available. However, we can't guarantee that they will always be there. If any isn't, a simple keyword search will take you to information about Glenn Gould and his music.

Photo and Art Credits

Page 40: Illustration by Chrissie Wysotski

Page 41: The Estate of Glenn Gould, photograph by Herb Nott

Page 43: The Estate of Glenn Gould

Page 45: The Estate of Glenn Gould, photograph by FedNews

Page 47: The Estate of Glenn Gould

Page 48: Illustration by Chrissie Wysotski

Page 49: The Estate of Glenn Gould

Page 50: Courtest of Walter Homburger

Page 51: The Estate of Glenn Gould, photograph by Paul Rockett

Page 52: The Estate of Glenn Gould/Town Hall Foundation

Page 55: Paul Rockett/The Estate of Glenn Gould

Page 56: Reprinted with permission—Torstar Syndication Services

Page 57: Courtesy of Sony Music, photograph by Don Hunstein

Page 58: The Estate of Glenn Gould/Department of Foreign Affairs and
        International Trade

Page 59: Napoleon Publishing

Page 60: Napoleon Publishing

Page 61: The Estate of Glenn Gould

Page 62: The Estate of Glenn Gould/Winter

Page 63: Photo by Chrissie Wysotski

Page 64: Illustration by Chrissie Wysotski

Page 65: The Estate of Glenn Gould, photograph by Paul Rockett

Page 66: The Estate of Glenn Gould

Page 67: Illustration by Chrissie Wysotski

Page 68: From the Walter Curtin Collection, National Archives of Canada

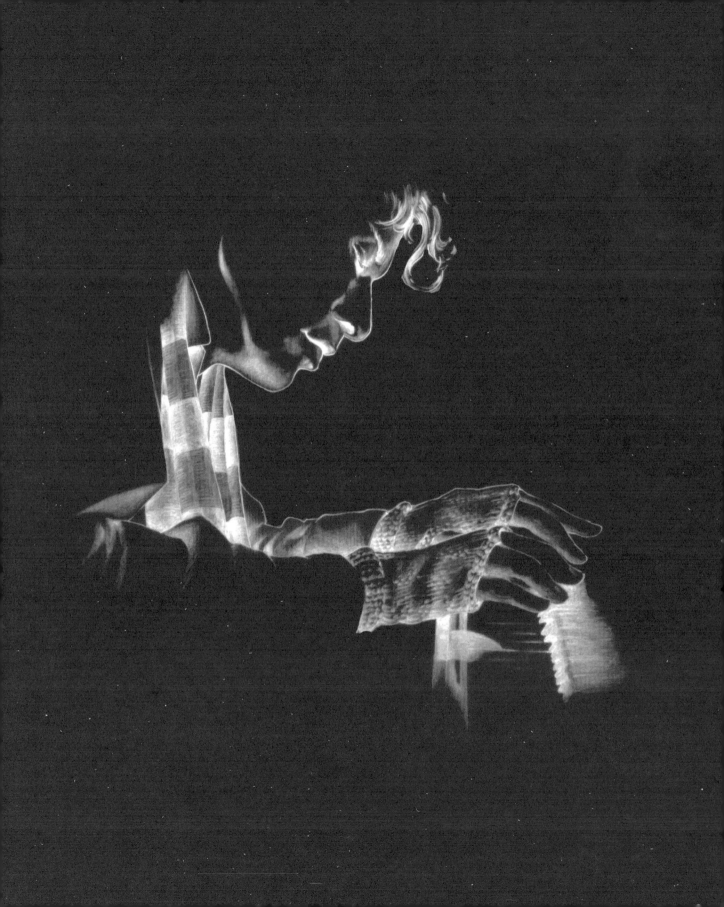